I Have to Get It Off My Chest

I Have to Tell My Truth

I0423593

Inguna Brazil

Strategic Book Publishing and Rights Co.

Strategic Book Publishing and Rights Co.
12620 FM 1960, Suite A4-507
Houston, TX 77065
www.sbpra.com

ISBN: 978-1-62212-963-8

Typography and page composition by J. K. Eckert & Company

Dedication

This story is dedicated to my family, friends, acquaintances, Irish pioneers, to every person who had to take up this heartbreaking challenge of emigration, people who fully reaped the benefits of harsh fate on their skin, and the harsh bread of hard work.

Also this story is dedicated to the families who are raising special children with special needs, and every day facing several difficult challenges and not giving up hope that one day a miracle will happen!

I wish to thank, you, my dearest family, my friends, my supporters, my publishing company, and all who helped me make it happen; to write this book, give it life, and get it published. I would like to say big thank you to my daughter's school staff for encouragement and emotional support in the process. Sincere thanks to all who have helped me make this happen!

All other people who have played a major role in my life and helped me make the right choices for my future. To the nuns of St. Joseph's and our parish priest—these wonderful people have selflessly devoted their entire lives to serving God and humanity.

Sister Maria-Theresa and Sister Joan were my friends and teachers. Sister Agnes has been a living example of charity, and Sister Elizabeth is the epitome of tenderness and compassion. She worked for many years as a hospital chaplain. She knows the pain and despair of bereavement.

Meeting with Father Williams-Pierre has changed my views on religion and faith. He helped me realize that religion and faith are not the same thing. Faith is not only a pragmatic assumption, and it has been the past dogma only in the Soviet way of thinking. It is a living, breathing, and actually existing powerful spiritual force. Faith is the lifestyle of thousands of Catholic families.

I saw it in my pilgrimage to Lourdes, travelling together with our parish members, volunteers, and medical staff. Thousands of people have gathered here from all over the world, Europe and America. It was a very impressive and emotionally fulfilling experience.

Lourdes Cathedral's roof is from gold poured and donated by the Irish people. Moreover, it is huge. Lourdes Shrine itself is very well maintained and kept. The surrounding town is a typical tourist town, beautiful and interesting with its ancient architecture and lots of cafés and souvenir shops. The town is full of tourists and pilgrims. The river has the clearest turquoise mountain water.

Our church parish priest and nuns living in our parish helped me grasp and believe that Jesus Christ is always beside me and is my eternal companion, as his love for me is immeasurable, without prejudice, and unconditional.

All around people are criticizing the church and religion, forgetting that the fault is mortal. Those were people, mortals, who abused their privileges to represent the interests of the orphanage, not the church itself, nor the faith in Jesus Christ.

I can say that my faith in God has helped me to survive disappointments, has given me hope, spiritual strength, and comfort at a difficult time. I am not sure whether alone on my own, with my own resources, I would have been able to withstand that.

Prayer has given me strength and hope in both good days and not so good. Christ's teaching has helped me to see and bring out the good in each day's events, providing training for the future, so the next time a situation arrives, I will be able to deal with it.

No matter how bizarre or strange it may seem, God has given us a very important life weapon—free will. By way of example, none of us are perfect, and it depends on how we perceive ourselves and our fellow human beings around us. Our lives are formed either as a small hell or blessing for ourselves, family, and friends.

A very simple example is a family with three children. One of them is a special kid with special needs, the wife does not work, and the husband likes to sit in the pub with friends. One family and two possible life perceptions and possible lifestyles, from his wife's point of view:

First: Oh, God, I am so unhappy within. Help me please! All on my own with three children, one of them sick, my husband all the time in the pub, and I am so unhappy!

Second: Oh, Lord, I thank you that you have given me my family and my husband, that I am not alone in this life. Lord, I thank thee that two of my kids are full of health, and when they grow up, they will be able to take care of their sick brother. I will have help and support from my children in the future.

Thank you, Lord, that you have given me my spouse, that we agree that we all need your help. We are only humans with our weaknesses.

God, I thank You, Lord that you have given us friends who are with us every day and on holidays, in our joys and sorrows. I am grateful that you have provided us with all the necessary needs.

We always have all in plenty. We have a roof over our head and nutritious meals on the table. Thank you very much for everything, for your unconditional love to my sick child, for my two other children, and for their health.

So ask yourself, what do you think the scenario you think people have the chance to live their lives happier and more harmonious.

The more we appreciate what we have and are grateful for it, no matter how much or how little it is, the more likely we will spend our lives being happier.

I am not saying to ignore problems or negative side effects—they must be resolved. I say, "Do not let the negative overshadow the positive, but the opposite: try to highlight the positive in order to reduce the negative impact on your life."

Since I live my life by this daily motivation, it has become more joyful. That does not mean that it is always all good, just as naturally weather has sunny days and cloudy days, like our lives have better days and not-so-good days.

Our entire life is a journey, and each of us has to survive its own destiny, and gain life experience. Established values always come in handy. At the end, it is called wisdom.

My family always supported me in all my endeavors, shared my joys, and consoled me in my sorrow and challenges. "Everything will work out for the best."

My late grandmother used to say, "God sees everything." She was a faithful Catholic, and as soon as Latvia regained its independence, she attended church every Sunday mass, to the last day of her life.

We each have been given free will, to follow the teaching of Jesus, or do our own thing. And not every time are we right or more accurate. We are only human, and humans make mistakes—it is part of human nature. Here is only one solution: either we recognize that we have made a mistake, ask Christ forgiveness of the offense, and if we ask for help, he will help us, or we can stubbornly insist on our own mind and ignore the obvious truth.

It would be foolish to imagine that after prayer God just comes down to the earth and will give you what you have asked for. Of course this is not how it happens in real life, but he definitely sends opportunity to change your life—you hear somewhere in the conversation the topic that is important to you at the moment, and you get to know people who can be useful in your needs and can help you solve your problem. Now, when you are thinking, oh, God, it is all completely hopeless, just from the thin air in front of you appears an opportunity to do something about it.

I say a big thank you to all who have given me inspiration and supported my efforts to write this story. Thanks to everyone who said at the end of our conversation, "You all should write it down and describe all these events in the book." Many people have no idea about these events. What forced Latvian people to leave their homes and loved ones, and go abroad to look for work?

Everything it considered the right and wrong, I said to myself, "Why not?" Here also is a great challenge. I have to write the story in my own language, and afterwards translate it in English. So I started to think it was worth a try. Sister Joanna said that writing is good for the soul and exercise for the brain.

To tell the story is much easier than to write it down, and considering the inspiration, I said to myself, "Why not?"

I had just completed a first draft in Latvian. I gave it to my sister to read, and asked her what she thought of the content. My sister said, "It is up to the reader to decide if he likes it, if it is his object of interest. We all have different hobbies and interests."

I leave the novel at the individual's own responsibility to like it or hate it.

In addition, I simply recount the events of that time from my own prospective. Moreover, I definitely know that thousands of Latvians in Latvia and abroad would agree with me that all of it was done deliberately, to destroy the lives of ordinary people. Now in Latvia 10 percent are rich, and 90 percent are poor.

The middle class is not born yet. People were trying to go back to Latvia, but many of them had to come back to Ireland or move to England, because they were not able to fight corruption and unlawful laws. You have to be ruthless to survive in Latvian business.

I think that people have a right to know what happened after the so-called perestroika, when all the old existing equipment was broken down, collective farms were run down to the ground, everything was looted or "privatized," the privileged class of "self-made millionaires" was formed, who had a lot, and new to Latvia were the unprecedented sort of poor, who had nothing, who never was there before.

It started when one day without warning monetary reforms were made, which severely shocked and affected ordinary people. All ordinary country folk were saving for a rainy day—let's say 1,000 rubles, for unexpected expenses, a funeral, maybe for a daughter's wedding. One morning, they woke up and in their savings accounts, instead of 1,000 rubles there was 5 lats, an amount of money that, well, would be enough if you bought enough food for one day.

People were shocked, desperate, ruined, because no one was warned. Moreover, none of them could imagine that something like this could happen.

Then afterwards there was the "privatization certificate vouchers affair." Every Latvian inhabitant was awarded a certain amount of privatization vouchers, depending on his age and amount of years lived in Latvia.

These privatization voucher certificates were expected to be a payment option so that people would be able to buy out their state-owned apartments in which they lived. Evaluations were made. A certain amount of privatization voucher certificates would be required for each apartment type, with or without facilities, gas, central heating, water, and would be required for each square meter of living space.

The monetary value that vouchers had was very low. To buy out a normal two-bedroom apartment would require a relatively large amount of vouchers. The average family with 2–3 children would have an insufficient amount of privatization voucher certificates at their disposal, depending on the average age of the family members.

They might have to buy extra vouchers in the stock market to add to the present certificates for buying out their accommodation.

On one hand, you could count the people who could be described as average, affluent, or well-off. The poor were forced to sell their privatization vouchers to make ends meet and meet basic daily needs.

At the same time, the wealthy bought up certificates (vouchers) in large quantities, privatized land, houses, and apartments that previously belonged to state enterprises. The poor were left only poorer, because they had no money, and the rich kept growing richer.

An elite class of professionals, bankers, director's executives, and bookkeepers owned the land, shops, banks, and apartment buildings.

They could be charged rent. Made a so-called "European standard repairs" and screw "European prices" mere mortals, these prices could not afford. Our so-called new rich "self-made millionaires" and businessmen enriched themselves at the expense of ordinary folk, scamming and robbing their own Latvian compatriot citizens.

Then began the denationalization affair. Latvia has quite a lot of buildings that were built before the Soviets overtook Latvia, ranging from twenty to forty years old, which were nationalized, and the owners were sent to Siberia, after being declared public enemies.

Either by moving them into the smallest flat in the house, the rest of the return of state-run. It was decided that the buildings would be returned to either the owners or their heirs.

Others came and looked at them, saw that they required sprucing up and investment, and drove away. The buildings were left unmanageable and turned into slums, and my mother lives in one of them.

Before World War II, the house belonged to the church. In Soviet times, it was the state's property. Now it had been given back to the church. The house was very old; church had no means to renovate it, and was looking to sell. The house started looking like a ghost slum.

My mother went to the city council to look for other accommodation. Their answer was, "That house! It is not the worst one. Other people have even worse living conditions in the city."

It seemed that not until that rotten floor fell in, and the broken chimney fell down, and roofs fell on people's heads, would anything be done.

The council housing section was happy that my mother had a roof over her head, and it did not care that the house was falling down. It was not doing anything about the safety of the people who were living there.

My mother's application that she made when we were small kids was lost in the archives—that was what the council officers were saying.

Other owners or their heirs came and looked at the property, and saw that the house had value still and the paying tenants living in tried to knock out more benefits. This instigated corruption and bribery. Everything was based on being important and having contacts "in high places." If you did not have friends in high places or anything useful, you were nobody. No one needed a simple little person or a simple honest worker.

I hope that maybe this little comment helps explain why so many immigrated to other countries.

We were no adventurers, seekers of a good life, or traitors, which is what some "patriots" called us. They said we were like rats fleeing a sinking ship, instead of rebuilding the country and bringing prosperity.

Our country's officials and newly made entrepreneurs had managed to put us out of our dreams and our ideals. They ruined our simple lives.

We did not leave just like that, just for fun. We were forced to go in search of opportunities to earn a living and provide for our families, because there was no room for us anymore.

The newly born Latvian businesspeople did not need workers aged 35–40 years. We were written off as useless, as retired tools. They were looking for "new opportunities" to attract customers.

This led to massive emigration, and people went to countries where they were needed. Latvians have always been recognized as precise and hardworking people. We are punctual, helpful, making our work with quality and the best of knowledge. Nobody abandons their work, and everyone agrees to do overtime, if it is needed. We have always been caring family people. The story's hero is one of the many who were forced to leave Latvia to seek employment.

Preface

I was born in the Latvian Soviet blooming heyday, when the Soviet Union was one of the greatest empires in the world. In the "Iron Curtain" time it experienced its height of prosperity, and then of course, like all other empires, crashed.

Our parents were firm, conscientious citizens of the Soviet Union; their entire life was devoted to public welfare.

Family and children had to come afterwards. Institutions of the state undertook child rearing. Parents were obliged their hearts and minds to spend time bringing up communism and national prosperity.

Brainwashing of children started in kindergarten and continued in school, technical school or university, and alternatively in the workplace. Lenin and the Communist Party were the replacement of God. Everything else was unimportant.

As soon as the children reached eight years of age, around the second grade, all of them were enrolled into the children's organization called "Lenin's grandchildren." We all were issued a star brooch with a portrait of Lenin in the middle. It was our pride and an integral part of the uniform. After, about 10–11 years of age, we all were admitted to the Pioneers, and given red scarves. The Pioneers slogan was—are you ready?—always ready! For each country's celebration, on the first of May, workers solidarity day, the ninth of May, victory day over Hitler, the twenty-second of February, army and navy day, the eighth of March, women's solidarity day, it was our duty to participate in public homage parades.

In the last year of school came the last stage of a young person. A flag-shaped badge was issued in the form of Lenin's head in a side view. This was the start of your career, if you were ready to fight in elections.

If you excelled at studying, though, there was a possibility that, if you were able to get the highest achievements in the whole Union, you would be included in the chosen numbers of talented kids to spend their summer vacation on the Black Sea special Pioneer camp, which was called "Artek." All the gifted children had been invited from all over the Soviet Union, who were accomplished in academics, sports, and music, who had the potential to represent the glory of the Soviet Union.

If you had a thirst for a political career, then you could try to become the executive secretary in primary organizations in the school, then the district, and then the republic level—if you had the backbone for it.

I was not included in those children. I did not have an overriding desire for a career at that time; I had not yet grown to that point.

Rather, I was a dreamer. I wanted to travel, see a foreign land and strange countries, and meet interesting people. I was passionate about travel storybooks. I was using every chance to read—in bed, before I went to bed, outside on the bench in summer evenings, and on the bus, if I was going anywhere.

Our relatives had "fled abroad" during World War II, so we were transferred to the politically unreliable numbers list.

My late grandmother never talked much about it. She said the walls have eyes and ears, and you can never know whom you hear, and who is listening. Spying was a common thing. We certainly could not accept this, being children. We were curious. Grandmamma said that we, the children, should not challenge fate.

Since they could get in our late grandfather's co-workers way. Of course, our curiosity had no boundaries, and we wanted to know what had happened to our grandfather's co-worker.

It has been more than forty years, and our grandmother's brief retelling is still alive in my memory: My late grandfather worked at the beginning of the fifties in a local factory cement plant. The majority of workers were imported Belorussian workers. After the war, people were brought into Latvia from other Soviet Union regions, by wagons. In this cement factory, a few local residents worked, including my granddad and his colleague.

One morning my grandfather's workmate came to work. At home they had run out of wrapping paper. Instead of going to the shop, his wife had wrapped her husband's lunch sandwiches into newspaper. At noon grandfather's colleague unfurled his sandwiches in the canteen dining room, took the newspaper, and began to read it.

On the opposite side of the newspaper was Stalin's photo. However, he did not see it, or did not pay any special attention to it. The newspapers were always full of "beloved leader" pictures. The midday break ended, and grandfather's workmate folded newspaper, threw it in the trash bin, and returned to work. That same day in the evening after work, he was arrested, right at the factory gate.

People were surprised. Granddad's colleague was accused of treason and contempt for the leaders. He was sentenced to twenty-five years in exile, and his wife of fifteen years in exile as accomplice. Afterwards no one was seen and none knew what happened to their family, or where they disappeared, and what happened to their children. At the time, we did not understand our grandmother's warning.

Now as a grown woman, I understand that my family first was concerned for our safety, when nothing was ever discussed in the presence of children. Therefore, we accidentally did not overhear something unnecessary. We were firmly cautioned that no one had to know what was going on at home, and what our parents were talking about or discussing.

Children were making friends with other children. We were cautioned not to talk to strangers, and in any case do not go up to play on another's playgrounds, and not to enter into another home. We always were sent out to play in the backyard during the day or to sleep to bed at night.

I have decided to attempt to write the story of my experiences at a time when it was very difficult to distinguish between truth and falsehood, wanting to know the truth, and ignoring it.

My grandmother was right when she said that good is everywhere and nowhere is bread without crust. Our relatives had immigrated to other countries, and after more than fifty years, we had not received any information from them. We did not even know if any of our relatives were still alive.

In the early nineties we got the news that my grandmother's brother and his family finally got to Australia in the early sixties. First they were sent to Greece, to the refugee camp, and then to Turkey at the end of the war, and then, finally, to Australia.

We were happy to know that they were all alive and healthy. I have five once removed cousins, three boys and two girls. They all were born in Australia, where my grandmother's brother and his wife had settled in Darwin.

Because I'm not very sociable person, and my circle of friends is not particularly remarkable, not celebrities or public figures, the story will be about normal, everyday people who were born in the former Soviet Union, brought up in the strict Soviet spirit, in simple average working families, and got the usual primary school education, without major success, or exceptional performance. Most of them began to work immediately after graduation from secondary school. Some went to technical school to learn a trade, and some tried "to break the ceiling" and get into the university.

Each of us lived our lives up to the moment of the start of irreversible changes in the so-called perestroika, and we still do not realize how much they turned our lives upside down.

I know that before me some authors have already written on this subject. However, each of us sees things differently, and this is my retelling and my way—how I see those events that induced the economic crisis affecting thousands of simple country people and children, the most vulnerable part of the population.

In my opinion, it was the most cleverly masterminded robbery of the century. The country was dismantled into pieces. A well-circulating, genius distraction system was invented to break down time into stages to collapse the country.

In addition, everything was carefully planned and done "legally." In addition, they got away with it. Instead of putting them away behind bars, those criminally oriented genius minds were called the "savers of the newborn country," celebrated, and praised.

I must confess, the subject is close to my heart. I myself have lived now in Ireland for decades, and I was one of those who left Latvia, dictated by cruel circumstances.

But I am very fortunate—I am here in Ireland, I met my spouse, got married, gave birth to my youngest daughter, and I'm very happy. I think of Ireland as my home—as they say, "home is where the heart is." My heart is here in Ireland.

Here are my children, my grandchildren, my husband, my friends, and my dog. In addition, my home—all that I have close to the heart.

During these years, several times I have tackled writing and gave up halfway. It all goes in a circle. And one day I was watching *Sister Act 2* on the telly, and actress Whoopi Goldberg's character was saying, "If you are waking up in the morning and you can't think about anything else than writing, you are destined to be a writer."

I began to write, quit, started again, again quit. It is hard to put the heart on the paper. It is difficult to present feelings that have been the motivation for such action.

Over the years people become smarter and calmer, and after a long time it is already much easier to assess the situation with a clear mind.

This situation is different; the same flame is still burning deep inside. There is resentment that we, the Irish Latvians, were forced to leave our homes, loved ones, and country and go abroad, to support ourselves and be able to keep our children fed, and to be able send them to school to get a proper education.

In order for Latvia to regain freedom, we went to demonstrations for freedom from the Russian troops, asking them to leave Latvia. And what did we get? Beggars Tarbes on our backs. Instead of Russian Biro crates we had to put up with our new "self-made millionaires." "Same crayfish just different color in another bundle."

In the Soviet time, the Communist party chiefs were condemned for visiting spas abroad, and having the best of the best. Is there something that has changed?

The same poor Latvian country man did not see any further than his backyard, but the new rich "self-made millionaires" traveled all over the world, and their children are getting the best education possible money can buy in high-quality schools and colleges abroad.

During the Russian occupancy time, working could not be avoided. If you wanted or needed to for some reason, you were able to work two and three jobs, if one salary was not enough for your family needs.

Low wages? In Latvia people are still working long hours for a handout of pennies. The only difference is that there is no work or retraining opportunities elsewhere, because there is no work in Latvia for simple country-man. That jobs that are still there are unpaid, or miserably low-paid.

Here people are evicted on the street, regardless of whether they have a place to stay. Because they are unemployed, and benefits are small, people cannot pay their rent to the property owners and cannot meet mortgage payments.

Officials say that the state has no responsibility for creating jobs; it is not a national responsibility to look after the homeless. What they should do? What are the state's and officials' responsibilities?

People have to pay taxes, but why? If a country does not take care of its citizens, on what merit is it entitled to get any taxes? For the government to put taxpayers' money in their own pockets? Then committees spending taxpayers' money for scientific research, what Latvians drives away from the Latvia. Why people are emigrating? The answer is plain and simple. States are ignoring their citizens.

Everybody knows a family who has "enjoyed" a taste of unemployment and poverty, and hopelessness, knowing that nothing will change for the better, as long as greed corrupted by power will be a key driver of those who are comfortably settled at the public purse.

Government seems to be living in another world, where nothing else exists than their interests and convenience. They are getting wages in one month bigger than professionals get in the calendar year. The only thing they are doing is filling up their own pockets. They do not care about anyone except themselves.

This time it is different. I perceive myself as a mature amateur artist enduring the agony of creation. In addition, there are the potential effects of my opinion. I am not afraid. I think you could find thousands of Latvian people who have the same opinion about our "self-made millionaires" who are dictating rules in the country, and the government that is implementing them.

However, let us keep an open mind. There is freedom of expression, and I do not do politics—that is not "my cup of tea" and it is not my intention to reclaim a new revolution.

I do not call anyone names; it is just my own opinion on the existing situation. I am not communist, or a member of any other organization, or a religious fanatic—just ordinary simple country folk.

Politicians, crooks, scampers, and businesspersons, rob people like me every day. We are their "scapegoats and milking calves." The only question is, "How long we will allow it to happen?"

The "volcano of creativity" resumed after a long sleep, and it is ready for a boiling lava eruption.

Everything that has accumulated breaks out. I know that this novel may well be the only story that I write in my life. Alternatively, maybe not—who knows?

It is a Latvian woman's life story, who, because of personal circumstances, was forced to leave Latvia in the nineties. Latvia experienced raging economic arbitrariness, and people were forced to emigrate in search of work, in order to protect their families, feed their children, and send them to school.

Many mothers and wives had the same dilemma every day—what to do? To pay the current electricity bill, or buy school shoes for a child— and both things had to be done. In many families at that time, one or both parents were unemployed.

Unemployment benefits were exceptionally poor—LVL 30 per month, one lat per day, and much more than this amount of money was needed to live, eat, and still pay the bills monthly.

One had to be a genius in accounting to balance expenses with incoming benefit money. One week a month people could cook the full meal or buy extreme necessities with this amount of money, but the other three and a half they lived on deep-fried potatoes with tomato ketchup and onions, and plain bread with margarine, borrowing money from relatives and acquaintances.

How long could it hold out? Many readers may not like these facts about the events of that time, but they are the real facts of history in those days.

I have always admired talented writers—Agatha Christie, Alexander Dime. I have always loved to read books. My mother used to say, "You have it read, and consumed." I have always wanted to write. During school years, when I was young girl, I used to write short stories—novels and fairy tales for the school newspaper.

1

Three years already without permanent jobs, doing part-time chores for miserably low payment, for a handout penny. Entrepreneurs in their own vanity no longer knew what they wanted—in their opinion, container harvester would require higher education, cleaners, waitresses; young, beautiful, charming, adorable, interesting, not older than twenty-five years of age. "Maid required, knowledge of foreign languages"—this was the most common job advertisement in the newspapers. It was interesting that a foreign language was required in order to read the floor detergent title, or in German to say, "Good morning" to a visiting German boss.

A nanny in childcare with a university degree—how much further money could go. Everything seemed possible if you had enough money to pay for it.

After all day chasing directors, executives, and shop owners, I came home, dropped the bag on the coach, and stood at the mirror.

At thirty-six years of age, I had not the slightest chance of getting any job. I was emaciated, or as my neighbor said, "Unseemly weak," with black circles under my eyes, and depression stamped on my face.

For three years I tried to find a permanent job, but without success. Even my fifteen-year-old daughter, Emily, started to complain: "Why can all the other moms find work, but you have nothing? You are just too proud to work."

I said nothing. I did not know why I couldn't find a job. In addition, I did not have the slightest desire to engage in any discussion on this subject. I was totally depressed. The only thing I wanted was to go to sleep and to not wake up the next day.

I was tired from the senseless trotting around the city, desperately hoping to find at least some kind of work, even the most idiotic. Wages were what really mattered.

Every morning, I woke up with the hope that maybe finally luck would shine on me today, and every day ended the same way as the previous—again, with nothing.

The next morning I started all over again. I got off the bus in the end of the city, at the big circle, at the business park, and visited all the companies in a row—it was hopeless and pointless, and without any success. By noon, I had checked out all the companies in the area—sawmills, a meat factory, and bakery workshops—nowhere to nothing.

There were polite faces, smiles, and promises: "If we will have any suitable position, we will contact you." I was at a crossroads. At the roundabout, in despair I prayed, "Oh, God, where are you? If you really exist, do something. Help me, I beg you, please. I do not have strength enough anymore, everywhere is like a stone wall. I cannot; I have no strength to tolerate this stuff. What can I do? I need work—I really need it. I have no one else to take care of me and my daughter, Emily. I cannot rely on my mother's pity for me for the rest of my life. Please do something, if you really exist, do something, give me a sign, a hint, no matter what, so I know that you have heard me, that you have listened to me!"

I slowly started to walk back to the city center. From here to the center would be some five miles. I put my hand into my jacket pocket and found another 5 cents. I would be able to take a bus!

I reached the bus stop and waited. Finally, the bus arrived. I got inside; the bus now ran only a few times a day, and it was overcrowded.

On the bench behind me, I heard two female voices. "Sweetie, do you know that Leo is back from the Ireland? He has established an employment agency, and is now recruiting people to work in Ireland."

I was listening carefully with both my ears. Hmm, that was interesting news. Ireland was full of all kinds of work. You could choose whatever you wanted.

"Monday he will start interviews in an old farm office." The woman shared the news with her friend.

I remembered Leo very well—we all worked together. He was the local agricultural office manager, Tamara was the executive secretary, and I was the youth foreign liaison officer. We all were good colleagues and friends.

I got off the bus. I thought to myself, thank you, Lord for the good news. Monday I would go talk to Leo. If I failed, that was one more humiliation, along with all the mess in my life. I was paying now the price for being weak.

At home I did not say anything, in order not to give my mom and my daughter false hope. They had enough worries already. Emily needed to concentrate on her studies. Three people, including me, were on my mother's LVL 30 monthly pension.

What a shame. It should have been vice versa. I should have been taking care of her, and she should not have been feeding my daughter and me from her small pension.

On Monday morning I walked down to the city center, to the old agricultural administration building.

Outside was a long queue of people wishing to apply for work, any work—all they wanted was just to work. I joined the queue and watched out for any chance to get inside the door sooner. After three hours, finally I was nearly at the building door. After two more hours, finally I had reached the cabinet door. "Next!" I heard a woman's voice. With a shaking heart, I went inside.

"Oh, God, have mercy on me, this is my final, last hope to break away from the vicious circle," I thought.

"Lola! You! What are you doing here? I thought that you have already gone abroad a long time ago!" Leo came towards me with open arms and embraced me, and I was in tears! "Well, now that there is a flood of tears, sit down; tell me, what is going on with you?" Leo looked at his wristwatch. "Mandy, now it is half-past four, and you can go home. Have an early evening. Tell the people outside that we are finished today and they can come back tomorrow. Tell them to draw up their own list for tomorrow, that the second time there will not be any unnecessary queue. Make us coffee, and you can go home." Then he turned to me. "Have you calmed down a bit? I really did not expect you to meet such conditions. You had everything—a brilliant career, apartment, husband, family. What happened?"

Leo poured us both a coffee, lit a candle, and waited. I was trying to pull myself together and calm down, and I started watching the candle flame. And there, in the flame was a small pixie, an angel—I do not know exactly what it was, but something was sitting in the flame, a small creature, and moving with the flames. I did not say anything, because I did not want to be in a compromising situation. Visual hallucinations! On the other hand, maybe I actually had visual hallucinations.

I slowly started my story. "Remember the summer six years ago, when we had Swedish farmers looking for collaborates in agriculture, meat and dairy products? The same autumn a farming youth worker cooperative exchange program was established between the Latvian and Swedish Young Farmers Clubs. Candidates had to withstand competition. I passed the competition and got into the lucky sixteen, of the fifty candidates, who were able to go to Sweden as exchange students to the university to study in the Swedish Youth Leaders course. The training was six months' paid scholarship. The grant was large enough for my mom to take care of my daughter, Emily."

Leo asked me, "But what about your husband?"

"Henry was very happy that my mom would take on all the obligations of parenting Emily," I said. "And it was one of my biggest mistakes."

"Mom was right when she warned me that distance and time alienate people. At that time, I did not feel it was important. I was excited. A study opportunity in Sweden seemed more important than what would happen with my family life and my relationship with my husband. To see a foreign country, meet new interesting people, get a foreign degree and qualification in a profession, and receive a scholarship—I was over the moon. I was very proud of my achievement.

"I spent six months in Sweden. I absolutely loved it. Our group was sixteen students, all from different youth organizations, ages 18–30. We were studying history, law, management, psychology, and outdoor activities, working on different projects. Study time was fulfilling and rewarding. We met interesting people; we visited Swedish Doyle, the Latvian embassy, and a radio station. It all was very exciting.

"After studying, I came back to work. I was full of ideas and future projects. The Department of Agriculture was inverting the cash management structure, implementing cutbacks on the staff. I was able to get my job back, but on a youth exchange program department managers voluntary basis, collecting the percentage of membership fees and events ticket sales, but without proper wages."

"You were already gone. I already had gone to Ireland to work," Leo told me.

"I could not afford to work as a volunteer and I gave my resignation. I went to work in the nearby nonurban, rural school as nonprofessional English teacher. I was given notice that I had to obtain a teacher qualification. As you know, I have always loved to study, and learn new things. I have always been easy to talk to.

"I started part-time university studies. During the sessions I lived in Riga, renting an apartment from our friends who were working and living in England. Saturday afternoons I was going back home. I was happy with my life, work, and studies. However, one Friday, afternoon lectures were canceled; a teacher had some sort of other urgent business. We were told that we could be free until the next session.

"Of course, I was very happy. I went to the apartment, threw my belongings in a bag, and rushed to the intercity bus to get home that evening. When I got there, it was late evening. The house was quiet, the windows dark, the door shut. I thought that no one was home, that Emily definitely was with her grandmother, and that Henry had gone somewhere with his friends, or went to visit his parents.

"I opened the door, put on the light, and went inside through the kitchen to the bedroom to change my clothes. I opened the door, and there in the bed with my husband was the upstairs neighbor, my friend! I could not believe my own eyes—it all seemed unreal. It could not be!

"Moreover, how do you think it all ended? Henry told me, 'It's your own fault—why did you come home? You ought to be home tomorrow!'

"I knew that he was lying to me, but something like this I had not expected. He could not even leave his wife's friend alone. He could not pass without seducing her and sleeping with her, whenever I was away. They were lovers, and they had an affair.

"Scarlet moved away, back to the other side of Latvia. She could not afford to be exposed, because she was a teacher. Rumors were spreading very fast. It would ruin her reputation. She tried to apologize to me for what happened.

"My surprise was perhaps as big as yours was today, when you met me; the only difference is that for me it was a very unpleasant surprise. Henry and I were trying to continue to live together, but between us had come an irreparable alienation.

"We became two strangers living in the same house. It seemed it did not help to be married 'for the child's sake.' We attended family counseling. I even agreed to take a hypnosis session to calm my nerves, because I hated him so much—to death! It was very strange to have these kinds of feelings. I have never felt like that in my life.

"Instead seeing myself with my husband, I saw myself at Calvary, kneeling at the feet of Christ. He was nailed to the cross, I was kneeling at his feet, and I cried, and cried and cried until my heart broke into pieces because of pain. When I came out of hypnosis, I was in tears like a child.

"Of course, all this had no result. I could not forgive him. I could not forget his incisive tone answering that I came home at the wrong time. My identity as a woman was offended. Okay, maybe I was not the perfect wife, but I had always treated him with respect and been reliable. I had never betrayed him at any time in our marriage, even though I, like he, had the opportunities. I was faithful to my husband, and I loved Henry. I never played unfairly against him.

"Yes, I might have focused more on my career development than Henry and my family in general, but I do not think that this is an excuse for the betrayal. Henry did not think that he had offended me or done anything wrong, or that he would have to apologize to me about the ugly incident.

"After a long trial, I won the divorce case, and he finally gave up. He was found guilty, and questioned by the court. He kept an apartment; I got custody over my daughter. An apartment for him—a child for me!

"Therefore, I was divorced, poor, and lonely, with a child. In any case, my financial and social situation turned out to be not so good. When I told the schoolmistress that my circumstances had dramatically changed, and for family reasons I would not be able to continue my studies, I was demoted. I was not regarded as the teacher any longer— just an assistant teacher, and hence the pricing of my wages changed from 135 lats per month to 80 per month.

"In addition, when the school was able to arrange a new English teacher, just after graduation, I was kindly informed that my services were not needed anymore. If I wanted to, I could stay in school to work as a youth program coordinator part-time, ten hours per month with a 30 lats salary.

"Tell me what I have to do. I left school and started looking for something else; work with some meaningful wages. FAS suggested that I move to Riga, the capital city, and look for work, that here with my qualifications and with an incomplete higher education there would be more opportunities to get a job. Locally there were not any available vacancies, and other than any of the other rural schools, where they needed foreign language teachers, they could not hire.

"I knew that it did not make any sense. It would be exactly the same vicious circle—go to study, if not, then work on the pence, and when will rapier someone with a university education, you will be no longer be needed.

"I went to Riga. I got a job, but life turned out to be very hectic. I got up at 6:00 a.m. in the morning to allow time to prepare for the job, to get ready, to get to the trolleybus stop, to get in a crowded trolleybus and travel to other side of Riga, to get to the company office. You either have to cut down on your social life to buy a new outfit for work, or attend a hairdresser, or cut down on purchases to pay for an apartment and utility bills.

"I was seeking a permanent job with better prospects. Finally, I was offered a job in the Foreign Affairs Ministry. The salary was good, but it required a Riga living notation. And again, bite yourself on the fingers, where you will take 500 lats to buy the passport record stamp. 5 lats cannot save, where another 500 hundred.

"Emily had to go to school. She had only two years left. Class placement for children from outside residential area in schools here in limited quantities everything broken down by districts, estates, residential recording. The next school that would be willing to allocate a place for Emily in her age class was three blocks away. To rent a two-bedroom apartment for my mom to live with us was not affordable.

"My mom also was not very enthusiastic about the idea of living in Riga. She never liked big cities, noise, flocks of people, crowded trams, trolleybuses and buses, and queues in the supermarkets.

"I was tired of fighting windmills. I returned to our own city. From that time, three years, I have been without a permanent job and with no steady income. Leo, please help me, for old friendship's sake. I need a job, no matter what, no matter where!"

Leo looked at me, his face reflected deep reflection "Lola," he told me, "I cannot promise you anything, but I'll try. This firm, this placement agency, is not mine, but belongs to people in Ireland, and generally the cost for recruitment, employer's retrieval, work visa formalities, and home security is 150 lats. Where you will get that kind of money?

"Now, I do not have any normal jobs, except to go pick mushrooms in mushroom farms. Think about whether you will want to do that with your education and abilities."

"Leo, there is no longer any education. With a couple of courses in management, teaching, office management, English, accounting, and project management? Six-month courses for youth organizations leaders. What there is capacity or ability, I do not know anymore, if I am told by people owning businesses, that I am too old and illiterate, to remove the dishes from the cafeteria table, or to wash the floor.

"Company accountants require at least five years' experience of working with the latest computer accounting programs, where you will take it, if you do not have any friends in high places and do not know anyone, so who would agree to employ you just in good faith?"

"I am willing to work whatever job, no matter where the key is, so I can earn money and provide for myself and my child, regain my human dignity, so I do not feel like unnecessary waste thrown away. I feel just terrible, and you, frankly, are my last hope."

Leo stood in silence. Although was not easy for him to decide what to do, he said, "Give me time to think! I can telephone to Ireland and talk to the people for whom I work. This may take some time, but then do not say that I did not attempt to dissuade you from drastic steps. In my opinion, you deserve something better, like a place in Burger King or a hotel. If you are willing to wait, I will try to arrange something."

"Leo, I cannot wait—I have no way out. What do you think? How long will my mother be able to tolerate the fact that I am sitting out of work, and what my brothers and sisters will say about it?

"If you have a real job to pick mushrooms, I will do it. For the money, I promise I will pay back the last penny—just please help me. I am willing to draw up a promissory note with a solicitor."

"God be with you. Come or call me on Thursday, to see what I can arrange."

"Thank you, Leo." I got up from the chair.

I looked at the clock, and it was already half seven. Mom was probably already worrying.

"Okay, I'll go. A big thank you to you." I went to the front door.

At home my mom said, "Where have you been missing all day?"

"Mom, Leo is back from Ireland. He is recruiting people for work in Ireland in the mushroom farms, and I will go to pick mushrooms!"

"Are you mad? Where are you going? What will happen to Emily? Where she will stay? A child has to go to school!"

"I think she could stay here to live with you while she finishes school. I will work and will send money home for her and you. Then later we will see."

"You're not contemplating to go there forever?"

"No, but I think maybe for a year, to clear the debts, save some money, and then come back home."

"And when are you supposed to leave?"

"Oh, I do not know! Leo thought that I had gone abroad a long time ago. He was very surprised when he saw me, and even more surprised when I asked him to arrange for me to pick mushrooms in Ireland. I have to go back to him in a couple of days, and then he will be able to tell me if I have any hopes of getting a job or not."

"Lolita! Are you really convinced that it is the only way out?"

"Yes, Mom, I think so. I know. Latvia has me already written off as scrap, worse than a pensioner. They will at least get an earned pension, and I am doomed to a humiliating handout existence."

"And what if there is no work in Ireland, what then?"

"I do not know! Look for opportunities to go somewhere else. To England, or Germany, no matter where."

"Oh, God, give the child at least some consolation." Mom shook her head.

On Thursday morning, with a trembling heart, I went down into the city center to a meeting with Leo. Crowds gathered in front of building, I was not the only one seeking a job—so were all in the queue. All needed work and everyone was ready to go to work, no matter where, and any work to earn their daily livelihood for their families.

"Good morning, Leo. Do you have any news for me?"

"Yes, I think that I have some good news. In Ireland, in the Midlands, is a farmer who needs a 37–40-year-old woman with knowledge of English, who would be able to translate his instructions to the other workers. The salary is paid by the amount of mushrooms picked. The employer provides a three-bedroom caravan with a common living room.

"You will have one-year work visa, provided by the farmer. Interested?"

"Yes, but of course, I am very much interested. When I could start work?"

"I cannot say definitely; it depends on how long it will take to process the working visa in Ireland. Here is a long waiting list for processing visa applications. It can take up to six months. Now to the documentation. If you are ready to accept this job, then I'd like you to take this form, and carefully read it, and if you are agree with the rules, to sign that you have accepted the job offer and terms and conditions within it."

I almost started to cry again, but this time they were tears of joy and relief. Deep inside my heart, I thanked our Lord Jesus Christ that he had heard my prayer, and helped me to break the vicious circle.

I carefully completed the questionnaire, signed to the terms and conditions, and asked Leo, "What will happen next?"

"Nothing, Lolita. Now go home and wait. When your travel documents will arrive, I'll give you a message or call, you can also inquire the same. Something has to come up in about four weeks' time."

All my life I never thought that the most difficult part would be this long waiting for documents to arrive. Time crawled like a turtle. I started to lose faith in myself. From the beginning with great enthusiasm, I was telling my relatives and acquaintances that I was going to work in Ireland. Acquaintances had already started to tease me: "Now, where is our great Irish explorer? Well, what you are still doing here? We thought that you were already earning the big money picking Irish mushrooms!"

Time was going very slow; at home, the atmosphere was tense. We were short on money, but everybody needed to eat; food had to be bought every day. Winter promised to arrive and to be a cold one. We needed firewood for the stove and gas for the cooker, and electricity bill had to be paid. There were so many needs. By time, my expectations dropped the confidence decrease.

In early February, I was not working, and I still had not heard back from Ireland about my visa. Mom said loud and clear that she could no longer afford to buy me cigarettes. I smoked like a chimney and was burning lot of money in smoke.

I, once again, was feeling frustrated. Again, I had let everybody down. Everything was delayed. No news from the Irish Foreign Affairs Ministry visa department. I went to ask Leo what was going on. Why was there no word from Ireland?

"Lolita, do not worry. Everything will be fine. Your employer has already submitted an application for your work visa, all processing fees already paid, and we just have to wait until the Immigration Department confirms the visa. In addition, there is this delay because every day they have to examine hundreds of applications. Please be patient. Everything will be fine, all right?"

"Yes, for you it is easy to talk—you have a job, you're busy, and you don't even notice the day fly. When you wait, every minute seems to be an eternity," I quietly thought to myself, but I did not say anything loud. I did not want Leo to think that I was an ungrateful creature, how most of my acquaintances were considered. I was just keeping myself to myself and that was all. Feeling little bit better, I went out the door, with at least some clarity, some glimpse of hope, and I slowly went downtown.

In the market, I met with Melanie, my former classmate. When we were kids, we lived in the same multistory house. Our parents were friends and neighbors; we went to the same school and the same class.

Ever before we two got married, we were best pals. Then life separated us for a while. Melanie spent two years working in Denmark as an au pair. She had a very nice host family, and she looked after two boys who were full of life and big rascals.

After that, she finished her studies, became a teacher, and was appointed as a campus supervisor. Now our girls went to the same school, and the same class—her Linda and my Emily.

Melanie: "Hi, long time since I saw you. What are you doing?"

Me: "Nothing in particular, but you?"

Melanie: "Nothing and everything. Now I am on maternity leave. I just popped out to buy milk for the baby and will go home. Linda is babysitting her little sister. I have to think of something for tea. My husband will be home soon from work, hungry, angry and tired. Nevertheless, I have spare time just now. We can have a fine chat, just like in the 'old good days'. If you are not in a hurry, then you can join me along the way."

We walked along the sidewalk, and remembered the good old school times, in sixth year.

That summer, our parents allowed us for the first time to celebrate St. John's feast in the summer solstice, accompanied by an adults. Of course, we had no sense of what we could not do; we got very sweet homemade honey beer and cheese. Mmm, sweet and tasty! The celebration beer and caraway cheese and small pork pie! Rest of the class wondered where all the left?

We had arrived at Melanie's home. "Are you coming in for coffee? You can look at the new baby girl."

"What you will call her?"

"Veronica, my grandmother's name."

I answered, "Yes, of course, I would love to see the new baby." Melanie put on a kettle. We sat at the table. Melanie said to me, "You look terrible, as if you are recovering from a serious life-threatening illness. Is everything okay? What happened? Tell me, what is going on with you?"

I could not lie to her, and did not really see a reason to hide what happened, so I said, "No, everything is twisted upside down. My whole life is pure chaos. I am left alone and divorced. I caught my husband in bed with another woman. I've lost my nerves and my career. I've turned into a rag. I've lost the two-bedroom apartment in our cooperative building after Henry retained it.

"After a lot of difficulty, I got the social housing administration to give me at least one room, in an alternative rent house. During the winter, I was put out on the street by the house owner, because I had no money to pay the rent.

"You probably know that our house was denationalized and handed back to the owner's heirs. The home proprietor is now the mistress. She is from Riga, and she put capital rental prices on the property. I had to go back to live with my mother. You can imagine, at my age, to move back with a parent-retiree.

"I've arranged to go to work in Ireland, and I'm just now waiting until the work papers come, but there is some delay in the examination, because of a large queue. But I do need the job and the money now, immediately. I do not have even so much as 20 centimes to buy myself a pack of cheap cigarettes. Well, my mother will feed my child and me. However, for how long?"

"Oh, Lola, oh, shame! Believe me, everything will work out. It will be all right, and do not lose courage and hope. Even in the worst, change is for the better. Believe me, and pray—the Lord sees everything, and if you will ask him to help, he will help.

"I do not have money to give to you, but I will bring up a few kilos of potatoes from the cellar, and share them with you. My mother's garden was a good berry harvest this year, with a full basement. I can give you some jam. My husband somewhere has a cigarette packet, and the both of you can split it and take a half of packet. He will understand! I am okay, I do not smoke."

I did not know how to thank her. Melanie was willing to share everything that she had at home. "Mel, what will your husband say about you dealing out your goods?"

"Nothing—we are Christians, and it is our calling and responsibility to help our neighbor in need."

Throughout my childhood, I lived in the same house with Melanie's family, but I did not know that they were Roman Catholics. At that moment, it occurred to me that God had sent these people, Leo and Melanie, to me, in response to my plea for help. I realized that he really existed. Moreover, I realized the truth: Knock, and the door shall be opened, ask and you shall be given. This was word of the Bible.

If you ask for advice or help, he will listen and answer your prayer. If I now say that my faith has always been strong, I would be lying. How many times have I questioned if he's heard my cry for help, how many times in moments of weakness have I been angry at him, that something has not happened as I wanted. But knowing that he was here, beside me, itself was giving me hope that everything would eventually work out, and everything would be fine.

A few days later, Leo rang me to say that my employer was going to call his phone number and he wanted to talk to me. I must be at Leo's workplace at ten for the telephone conversation with my next boss. After the phone conversation my employer was satisfied, and on February 28, I received a certified copy of a work visa and tickets to Ireland.

2

Good-bye, Latvia! Hello, Ireland. My departure from home, Mom, and Emily was a happy event. The hardship was over. The long waiting period was over. We all three were happy that the nightmare was over once and forever, and that our family once again would begin a normal human life. I would able to work, earn, and send money home, pay off my accumulated debts, and provide for myself and my family's living. I would work—it sounded like the most beautiful music to my ears.

My trip to Ireland led through Prague. Prague is one of the most beautiful cities in Europe. I could have wandered through the old streets for hours, admiring the beautiful architecture created by the cathedral and houses. Shop windows were filled with the most beautiful crystal products, from miniatures to giant vases and chandeliers, charms and precious stones.

First I flew from Riga to Prague, and then I had to change to a transfer flight to Dublin. I arrived in Dublin late in the evening. I came through customs and started watching for a poster with my name on it.

The language sounded very odd with a strange accent, and I realized that I did not understand it; it was so different from what I studied in school and in Sweden. Yes, I did know that I was in Dublin, and that it was Ireland, and I knew that it was English, but I was starting to worry

17

about ending up trapped. It is disaster if you are in strange country and you do not know the language and can't communicate, because you do not understand what people are saying to you.

Finally, I saw a young person holding a poster with my name written on it. I went in his direction. He said something in his slang very quick. I asked him to repeat one more time, but slowly, so he repeated what he said before, just very slowly. He laughed and said slowly, "Welcome to Ireland! I will drive you to your new place of residence."

Outside it was dark, and I had no idea where and in what direction we were going. However, the road was very smooth and wide and the lights shone all the way. The trip lasted about five hours, at least it seemed to me, until we stopped at a large two-story house with the lights on. "So, here we are," the person said in his peculiar English accent. He got out of the car and called at the door.

The door opened, and we step into the light, through a long corridor, and into a light, spacious room. We were in a large, wide kitchen.

This was the first time in my life I had seen such a big kitchen. It was almost the same size as my old high school kitchen. In one corner stood a distinctive appliance—a large green dual heating stove with electricity and diesel. It was strong, able to heat the whole house. The top surface could be used the same as a hob for frying and cooking. The stove had two built-in ovens for baking.

In the kitchen, a young couple around thirty years old greeted us— they were my employer and his wife, Michael and Lisa. They introduced themselves to me and politely asked if the trip was enjoyable. They offered a cup of hot tea after the long and tiring road. My driver kindly excused himself and said that he was going back to his home, wishing me a happy stay and good-night.

Lisa handed me tea. She asked if I took milk and sugar. I had never heard about drinking tea with milk and sugar in Europe—only in Far East Russia, far away in the mountains and Siberian forest. I took the first sip and was stunned. I did not know what to do. A terribly bitter, strong taste took over my mouth. Never in my life had I such strong tea.

I politely asked for milk, and it tasted good. Now, what would be the next surprise?

We exchanged a few courtesy phrases with each other, and wished each other good-night. Michael went to the room and Lisa came with me to show me my new place.

Bypassing the round building, we came to the small cabins. Lisa opened the door and pointed me to another door, saying that it was my bedroom. I opened the door to a small room, very compact, but inside was all that was required: a bed, wardrobe, mirror, TV, table, and inside a fridge. Lisa wished me a good night. I was very tired and just put my head on the pillow, instantly falling asleep.

I was entering a new stage of my life. I hoped it would it happier than the previous. We would see what tomorrow would bring.

I had a dream of a wedding in the church. Well, it was my wedding. All around people were talking in English. I was standing next to the groom, a stranger, and he spoke to me in English. We were holding hands as we left. Outside stood a woman in black, and I could not see her face. She was kind of invisible. The church was big and impressive, gray, built with stone bricks. The tower has a cross. It was very distinctive, but not like anything I had seen before.

I was awake, and outside the window the sun was shining. I did not know how long I slept or what time it was. I remembered my dream! They say that dreams come true, seen in strange place in sleep! Today I had to unpack, and then I would know the time. Somewhere in the suitcase was an alarm clock.

I heard voices outside whispering. I got out of bed and opened the door. "Good morning," I said, entering the lobby and the living room.

"Good morning, good morning," answered three women and a youngish man. "How was the flight? What time was it? Did you bring cigarettes and coffee with you?"

Stunned, I looked at them. Nobody told me that I had to bring cigarettes with me. Weren't cigarettes produced here in Ireland?

Everyone started laughing. "Now we can see that you know nothing about life here. No, cigarettes are produced here, but they are very expensive and we are deep in the countryside, 25 km from the nearest town and 5 km from the nearest village store.

"But don't worry—since you've just arrived, then it means that either Michael or Lisa today will take you to the city to shop for yourself. You will have to do the shopping for your first week."

"But I have no money," I quietly mumbled, shamefaced.

"Oh, you do not worry about it," the young man answered. "You will be given an advance—100 Irish pounds, and then afterwards Mike deducts it from your wages. And, yes, my name is Robert, Robby."

And the women told me their names: Anne, Rose, and Diana.

"Okay, but either way, the clock says 10:00 a.m., and breakfast break is over, so go back to work. You have your breakfast and join us. We left the breakfast sandwiches for you."

"What is your name?" blackish Diana inquired. She was a very pretty young woman, slim, tall, pretty, with a model's appearance.

"My name is Lolita," I said.

"Well, we will be in tunnel number four."

And the whole bunch of workers went out. I carefully looked around. It was a galley type of kitchen, with a living room, hall and two doors down. Aha, so I would be not in my own in here. There were two other flatmates. I looked out the window—there were meadows all around, and you could see cows grazing.

I had a sandwich, drank a cup of coffee, and went out the door. Gone out and watch which way would be the path I seen. In the front of something big, green, they said the tunnel, so this could be one of them.

Bypassing the circuit, I came out in the front of a large concrete yard. Here you could see a row of eleven large green tunnels such as greenhouses, but many times larger, with big double doors, each painted with a number.

On the opposite side of the yard and farm building there was a shed for workers, and next door was the chilling room for mushrooms in order to keep them fresh as long as possible. I counted all the doors in a row, to four, and went in that direction.

There at the door I met Michael. He said good morning in an interesting, previously unheard accent. It turned out to be the so-called "bog accent." The district is inland, and rich in peat bog, and the local dialect is known as the bog accent.

He quickly said something to me, and I was once again forced him to ask to repeat everything, slowly, word by word. I explained to him that it would take some time for me to get used to his speech. Mike determined that it was nothing and that I understood everything very well. We both continued the conversation, slowly approaching the tunnel.

Michael opened the door and there I saw an amazing sight. I would call it one of the wonders of the world. The mushrooms—white, small heads—were grown in heated, dark greenhouses. The view was unique. There were three rows, three floors, and frames of sachet fungi, as lettuce, cucumber, or everywhere shone white heads, more smaller, and very tiny, tiny.

Along the edges of the interesting carriers with the seat and flat shelf in the front. Each seat, adjusted for sitting, and with your feet, you push it forwards.

Each mushroom picker had a semi-circle knife, with which the fungus was cut off and placed in a box. The shelf had three boxes, each targeting different sized mushrooms—large, medium and small. There were even two adjoining smaller sizes, with different types of boxes, like a flat boat, for random mushrooms, whereas the basket was for buds, called buttons, small, unopened mushrooms.

For the top floor of the scaffolding, which was a platform on which to pick mushrooms while standing and with your arm and your body weight pushing moving forward?

Michael presented me with mushroom picking technical principles. Lisa would bring me to the city, showing me shops, and help me shop for the first time, so I knew what to get in the future. For me, it was something new, to shop for a week; I had never done so in all my life, even in the "good old times." Those who wanted to go to town could pick the big mushrooms in the morning and later in evening.

The farm was located 25 km from the city, in our Latvian perception in the middle of nowhere, but it looked like it did not bother Michael and Lisa. They said that it was nothing special, just twenty minutes by car to the city. And they liked to live in the countryside, because it was quiet, away from the city noise and crowds, in the fresh air. We were going to a city, quite sizable, about as big as Riga, called Shannon.

I really liked this city on the riverbank. We drove up to a large shopping center—Tesco. It was a large supermarket. It had everything from toilet paper to scissors and even household appliances—food, household chemicals, clothes, shoes, everything under one roof.

There was even a pharmacy on the second floor, several clothing stores, bookstores, cafés, news agents, and a "Burger King."

Now I understood what Leo meant when he was offering to find me a job in McDonalds, Burger King, or a hotel. Life in the city, work in the city center, eating there on the spot, the salary stays in your pocket.

Overtime paid a double fee. "Leo, thank you, I know that you are my true friend and want only the best," I thought. I guessed that one day when I recovered my human dignity, I might be able to work in the city, but in the meantime I was happy to get a job on a mushroom farm. It would be my soul sanatorium.

Little by little, gradually, without haste, I would build my life from scratch. I still had all my life in front of me. First, I had to get rid of all my financial problems. Debts had to be paid off, my nerves had to be put back it in order, and then, afterward, I could think about the next step.

I had to emotionally process all the new information that had come my way. Everything was new, and everything happened for the first time. And everything was in English. And unshakable peace that is quite possible to me because I am used doing everything quickly.

I coped with my first shopping. I spent almost all of the 100 pounds. I never thought I would still need so much. The next problem was where to put all the products. We had a refrigerator in the caravan; I did not believe there was enough space. It turned out that my TV cabinet had a refrigerator inside.

However, most of my money was spent on cigarettes. I would try to quit smoking, and coffee. Now I was not surprised that my colleagues wanted cigarettes from the Latvia. The difference in price was huge—good cigarettes cost 60 centimes in Latvia, but here they cost 4 pounds and 75 pence. It was a terrific difference. One Irish pound equaled 70 cents, and thus one pack of cigarettes cost nearly three lats—five times more expensive!

Little by little, I became more familiar with mushroom picking techniques; the work was simple, repetitive, and tedious. It had been a month since I started working, and now I was entitled to my first vacation.

For Easter, I had no special plans. Michael asked me how I planned to spend the vacation; I said that I wanted to see Dublin. He warned me to be attentive, because there was so much to see, but it was very easy to get lost. Dublin was a great city. I told him that it was nothing and I was not afraid. If I needed something, I would ask for directions from people passing on the street.

Early the next morning, I got to the airport bus. It was going straight to Dublin. I was getting a bit worried whether I would be able to manage on my own. After all, I had been in Ireland but a very short while—only six weeks.

It was not my first time abroad. I had spent a whole six months in Sweden, and three months in Australia. However, I felt like a child, going on my first adventure after a long illness.

Dublin surpassed my expectations. It was a majestic city with its city center and shops, theaters and cinemas. The post office and the main street were identical to the post office and main street in Melbourne. In the middle of the city flowed the riverside canal. On other side, it looked like the old town, with a castle and parks. There were deco-style buildings.

The day passed quickly, and it was time for the bus to go back home. I knew that this was my first trip to Dublin but not the last. I loved Dublin. This tour helped me cheer up. I felt that my spiritual strength was slowly returning. My spiritual recovery was underway.

Three months later, it was June. At Emily's school graduation, I felt proud that I finally was able to send my mother enough money so Emily could buy a suitable dress for school graduation.

Of course, I wanted to be there for her graduation, but I did not have a paid holiday yet and the plane tickets were very expensive. During this time many people were traveling to Latvia for children's school graduation. And I still did not want to use the paid flight back to Latvia, because who knew when I might need it. After three more months, in September or October, I would be able to travel to Latvia to pay back half of the loan to the Leo, visit Melanie, and thank her for her support at a difficult time. And I would spend at least a few days with my daughter, mother, and other family members. This time I would not be dependent. I would be able to throw a small party for my family members.

After my leave and visiting relatives and friends, I was happy to return to the mushroom farm. In Latvia nothing remained for me. My friends and acquaintances were scattered, and most like me had gone to work in England, Germany, Ireland, or somewhere else, like Denmark, Sweden, and Italy.

The city was empty, with only pensioners and underage children left. My sisters and brothers had moved to Riga and Liepaja. There was at least some kind of work for the lowest wages.

I offered them an opportunity to reflect on a job search in Ireland. When you have one of your family there, it is much easier to find a job.

My mother protested that it was not enough that I myself had gone away, but I was encouraging others to leave the country too. I asked my mother, "And it's good for them here? Long hours, low wages, hard work."

"Remember that when I broke up with Henry and I went to the city council, asking them to give me a separate apartment, the social housing officer said that I had to think about this before left my husband. I was not entitled to anything.

"When I asked why they could not speed up your apartment application, because we would be forced to live with you, the answer was that my mother's apartment application had been moved into the archives in the basement a long time ago. Placed in the archives?!

"How much ridicule I had to endure to win the case to get one room in a communal apartment.

"I have a chance to save up some money, which would help me do something, to start my own business, or buy an apartment for myself and my daughter, to give my child a chance to get an education and secure her future, so her life would be easier. I do not think you wish your children and grandchildren to have slave life."

My mushroom time came to an end. Michael asked me what I wanted to do next. Would I stay for another year picking mushrooms, or would I go home? I said that I am still not sure what would be the right thing to do. I had not decided yet what to do, but one thing I knew for certain—I was not going back to Latvia.

In the meantime, I bought my very first cell phone. In addition, I bought a small TV, which helped me with my English language acquisition and training.

Michael said that if I wanted to stay for another year, then he must be prepared in advance and submit the documents for my work visa renewal.

I was not sure if I wanted another year of picking mushrooms. I did not mind it, except for this dreary daily rhythm, and the work of eternal twilight with artificial light bulbs. I got up at 4:00 in the morning; the best mushrooms had to be picked until noon, so that the driver could to take them fresh to the station and transfer them. Then I would pick the rest of mushrooms.

In the afternoon, I did the so-called thinning. It was very demanding and intensive work, but not profitable, earning only 22 Irish pounds all day long.

Picking mushrooms is similar to the work of milking cows on a farm. Just as a milkmaid milks cows when the cows are full with milk and the animals have to be fed every day, the mushrooms have to be tidied and picked when they are ready.

All days were the same. There was no difference between Saturdays, Sunday, or a normal working day. The local farmers had entered into an agreement with each other. If a farmer did not have mushrooms, the farmer would send his workers to other farms to help pick mushrooms if neighbors need a helping hand.

In this manner, we were grouped with other mushroom pickers from other surrounding areas. All together there could be some fifty Latvian and Lithuanian workers, and three Estonians. Some of them had been working here for 2–3 years, which was easy to understand. It was not worth the ride home, because there was nothing to do there.

To be able to find another job in Ireland a person needed English language skills, or you had to be in a so-called deficit qualifications demand profession.

I tried to tell Lisa that I would love to stay here in Ireland, just get a little bit better quality of life. I would love to live in a nearby town. I would be happy to live there, but I would like to do something different, to work in a café, Burger King, or a store in the city.

I was trying to say it slowly to Lisa. She worked as a credit inspector in a bank in Shannon. Lisa was a well-respected woman and an acquaintance of many important people, and I wanted to ask if she could give me a recommendation. Probably in Lisa's eyes, it all seemed unreal.

She seemed disbelieving that I might be able to do some other intellectual work. Lisa did not understand what I wanted. Of course, I understood her very well—dressed in workout gear, rubber boots up.

I could not imagine anyone sitting at the counter in a clothing store or at the bank or at presenting the keys behind the desk in such an out-fit. It would look unusual and bizarre. I thought again, and resolved to get closer to my intended target.

I decided to talk to Diana. It seemed that her perception of life coin-cided with mine. I knew that her contract was ending, and I was inter-ested in what she planned to do next. I was happy when I discovered that she was also thinking of staying in Ireland and another job search.

I knew that I could not go back to Latvia. I needed more time to make more money. I still had to pay back another half of my debt to Leo. Emily had just started her studies in technical college.

All of this cost money. No, I had to work for at least another year, if not longer, until everything fell into place. Then maybe I would be able to start thinking about going back to Latvia. My sister was considering coming to work in Ireland. I received a letter from her asking to look for work for her. I knew that the neighboring farm needed mushroom pickers. I made a phone call to her and asked, "Would you be willing to go pick mushrooms?"

"But of course," she said. "But I do not have to pick mushrooms all my life. Something better will turn up, right?" I liked her voice. It was so childish and sweet.

I went to Michael and asked him to help me arrange work for my sis-ter at a neighboring farm. Michael asked me, "Does this mean that you will stay as well?"

I honestly answered him, "I'll stay until I find another job."

He said, "I like that you're honest and open. I will make a deal with Frederick about your sister's work, and I hope I will not regret it."

"No, you will not regret it."

Daniela was very gifted and she was a very good worker. She quickly grasped everything, and she had the artist's touch. Daniela was a painter, but during this time in Latvia, nobody could make a living with painting, except celebrities and famous artists, so she decided to come here to Ireland.

Robert said, "Your sister will be all right—she has you. Tell her that she does not have to worry."

Diana and I decided that in our spare time we would look for work together. That was also safer. Two heads together were better than one in a strange place, just in case we had to remain overnight at the hotel. In our search for work, we were confronted with an unforeseen obstacle—the work-permit visa.

Many employers were willing to hire us immediately, the next day. But after saying that we needed a work visa, a prospective employer's optimism disappeared and we had to listen to a hundred and one excuses—it was too costly, too complex, workers were needed right away and not after six months, they could not wait so long, and so on.

We wore a confident mask in the beginning. We decided to seek the help of local Latvians, because we were all in the same predicament.

It was another country, another language, and another culture. In the middle of the still hard work, long hours, causing for some people depression and nostalgia. Many workers left behind a husband or wife, and grieving children and families.

It was important to have friends, somebody to talk to in difficult times, someone who understood you and cheered you up when you felt let down. It is human nature to fear the unknown and unfamiliar. We all came here to work and we did not know for how long. The future was unknown.

We exchanged phone numbers, in case of emergency or for getting together for going out to a party, pub, or nightclub. If anyone was traveling back to Latvia, it was an opportunity to send a gift home.

We asked our comrades for a favor: "Please, if someone somewhere hears something about any vacant employment in the town or city, let us know."

3

In the beginning of November, we got the message that on the other side of the Shannon, in a local nursing home, the village Clonross was looking for nursing assistants and nurse's aides. We both went there for an interview. It turned out that work visas were not a problem, because nursing assistant was on the shortage occupation list. We could start work immediately. We were very happy.

Compared to the mushroom farm, the nursing home was the jackpot. It had large, bright rooms, long corridors, old-fashioned, expensive furniture, and ornate mirrors. Patients' rooms were bright, modern, and clean. In one wing of the mansion was a convent.

The nuns were willing to help us with a free room in the convent until we found something in the village, a house or rooms for rent.

It was a difficult task to give the sensitive news to Michael and Lisa that we had found another job. They really had treated me very well, and had been my first helping step towards a new life.

I actually felt a bit uncomfortable in front of them, because they even helped my sister to find work, but I hoped that they would understand me correctly and not condemn me for quitting before the end of the contract.

The mushroom pickers were now nursing assistants (nurse's aides). Working conditions were excellent and clean, and we were fed and had uniforms. Moreover, we were living for free until we found something suitable in the village.

Boarding House was a former large manor house with over 100 hectares of land, orchards, vegetable gardens, greenhouses, and sheds. Prior to the convent, nuns cultivated the land themselves and managed a boarding school. Now there were homes for the elderly and the sick.

The nuns sold the manor nursing home to the owners for the right to spend their retirement there until death. They were all already old, retired from active service, but they were all brisk and vivacious. It was difficult to determine their ages, but all of them were over seventy, and the Danish sister was already over ninety. She was the oldest, but no one could tell that she had reached so great an age.

The nuns were warmhearted, empathetic, and comforting. They had spent all their lives away from home, working in Africa, South America, and India, on nursing and teaching missions. They were no strangers to sad moments when you cry in silence inside you. I wanted to be at home, but I knew that it was my duty to be here, to work, to send money back home, and take care of family back home.

I could not let a momentary weakness affect my senses because my family's well-being and life depended on me. And my little sissy was my responsibility here in a foreign land, because she was here, and she had no one else's shoulder to cry on.

Payment for the work in the nursing home was much better. I was being paid for hours worked, and I could not complain about lacking a job, only the fact that Diana worked different shifts and different days, and we did not see each other very much. I got to work on my English a lot.

Here the elderly people had their own way of speaking, in slang; English was mixed with the Irish local expressions. However, fortunately, my work colleagues understood, and if I did not understand something, then I could ask my colleagues what that word meant, or what that person wanted.

When I could not find anybody else, I could ask my supervisor, Elaine, to give me a hand and go to the patient, so she could listen to what they were saying to me and then explain to me what this person wanted.

The technical service staff was composed of a few men. They were responsible for the nursing home technical side, water supplies, electricity issues, and equipment and transportation issues.

I noticed that one of them, Andy, had some interest in me. When he saw me, he always had a smile for me like sunshine. I had worked my first full week, and now I would have two days free, my first days off. At break, we all were sitting at a table and drinking tea.

Drinking tea was very popular, as well as Latvian coffee breaks. During tea all the local news and rumors are discussed—who died, who had a baby, who got married, and future actions. The girls were asking me what I had decided to do during my first days off. I admitted that still I really did not know. I wanted to look at the village, go to the city, walk through the stores, look around, and do some window shopping. I would send money home to my family. My colleagues asked whether I wanted to go out in evening, or go to the local pub.

My answer was that probably not, because I did not know anybody. Some lads sat at the next table, and I had no idea that they had been following our discussions. Andy turned to me and said, "If you want, I'll join for you a company." I gladly accepted the offer, and we talked about what time Andy would collect me at the door.

It was now my first date in Ireland, and with an Irish person.

It turned out they assumed that the evening is scours all existing pubs in the village. In addition, to my surprise, there are four taverns. The evening passed quickly. Andy was born and raised in the village, went to school here, and now works here. It seemed to me that there was no one he did not know.

People were very nice, very friendly and amenable. Seen has already spent not so good times. Andy accompanied me back to the nursing home.

Andy asked me if I would spend another evening with him having fun. I said that yes, I would love to spend another evening in his company. Andy asked me how long I thought I would live at the nursing home. I said that we wanted to rent an apartment in the village, but our quest had not been successful. We had not found anything. Andy promised to talk with his acquaintances about any house or apartment that could be for rent. He said that if I ever needed something, or had any problems, I could probably turn to him for help.

I was touched. Andy had a very nice nature, and he was a very empathetic, sensitive, and pleasant man. He was a little shy, but he had delightful, warm smile.

I wondered if he had a girlfriend. I had noticed that here they were slow to establish a family. As in Sweden, first came the acquisition of education, career, financial security, and then and only then, was one meant to start a family.

Couples were friends for many years, very often courting from the beginning of school, and then came the long-term engagement, and then to the wedding.

Marriage was very important for life in Ireland, as a strongly oriented Catholic country.

The next morning, I went for a walk in the village. Clonross was a nice, idyllic village, green, not too big, not too small. In the middle of the main street of the village was the road to Cork. Traffic was alive with cars, cargo containers, and buses.

The village had two supermarkets, a butcher shop, two clothing stores, two pharmacies, and four pubs, which was quite a developed sales network for a village.

When you were walking among the trees, you were in another world. Green Park had an open view of the river, countryside, and distant mountains, which looked blue in the distance. There was a peculiar silence and peace, and it was hard to imagine that there was the final avenue of highway, with continuous traffic.

I really liked this neighborhood, with a puff of green trees, the smell of the river, and the birds singing. There was silence, peace, and fresh, unpolluted air.

The center of the village overlooked the church tower, and I decided to walk there. I had always been fascinated by beautiful buildings, historic sites, antique furniture, paintings, and churches. I had often been told that I was born at the wrong time and the wrong place. I had always loved beauty, in art, nature, and life. Watching a touching love melodrama, my eyes are always wet, crying with the movie.

I was now at the church. From the outside it was very similar to the cathedral that I saw in a dream the first night, when I came to Ireland and was sleeping in a new location. I opened the church door and went inside. There were quite large mosaic windows, high wooden ceilings, and carved walls. At the very front of the altar was a window with a mosaic structure. I stunned look at it and did not believe my own eyes. The mosaic was prominent in the center, with Jesus Christ of Calvary, on either side there were angels, and at his feet was nestling Mary Magdalene, kneeling, embracing his legs.

Looking around, I was confused. The same view of what I witnessed and felt the hypnosis session twenty years ago, and which I could not find an explanation, and did not know what it means.

Now, this painting was in front of me, in a small Irish village, in a quiet church altar window. It was all incredible.

And some said God did not exist.

I was a witness to the fact that he had brought me here, that twenty years before he gave me a sign that I did not understand at that time, and without being able to understand, I ignored it.

Now I knew why I was unable to find work in the last three years. My place was here! It was fate.

To me it easier to learn English from the abbess's appointed teacher, Sister Mary, who helped me with the language and negotiating the acquisition of expression. We developed a friendly relationship, and I decided to share my emotional experience with her.

Sister Mary said to me, "What do you think why you are here? Do you really think that everything that happens in your life is just a coincidence? No, my poppet, it is God's will that has brought you here. It means that he has a mission plan especially for you, a mission that you have to fulfill."

I listened, and finally asked, "What is a mission? However, I am not even baptized."

"But do you believe that God exists?"

"Yes," I replied. "I believe that he is, and that he is there."

"Why do you believe?"

"Because I know, because I've seen that he has answered my prayers in my time of despair." Well, I had a question. "What do you know about Jesus? I've read the Bible, and when I was in Sweden, in my course was a girl who was studying at the Faculty of Theology, and she told us much about Jesus' life on earth."

"But would you like to know more about Jesus?" Sister Mary asked me. I said yes! Sister Mary invited me to attend a local church service in the chapel, right there in the nursing home. Services were held every morning at 10:00 a.m. But I never had the time, as usual.

One morning in the lobby, I ran into a tall, loud young man. He might have been around thirty years old and was stately. He wore jeans and sports boots and was bursting with health and vitality. The guy asked where he could meet the abbess.

I said that I would show him the way to the convent. Here she came down a long corridor. The young man introduced himself to her as a priest, Father William. The mother of the convent kindly asked whether he had a French ancestry. William replied that yes, his great-grandfather was a Frenchman. And his mother had named him Pierre-William in honor of his great-grandfather. I stood, nailed to the floor itself, not knowing why. I never imagined that he would be a pastor. Finally, I told the abbess that I was leaving their company. I had to go, and I would soon have to be on duty. Abbess introduced me to the pastor, saying,

"This is our new nursing home worker, a nurse's aide. Her name is Lolita and she is Latvian."

William laughed and said that he had a very bad memory for women's names and that he was calling all the women Mary.

I politely said good-bye and went to the nursing home facilities. My idea of pastors was shaken. As a child, I was accustomed to watch Soviet-era movies in which the pastor was an old, prejudiced servant. An old man about seventy years—that was my idea of a priest. Moreover, here in front of me stood a young, attractive, cheerful, and humorous man and he was a pastor. It definitely did not match the image of the priest who inculcated us during my school years.

I began to realize that everything was very different than what I was taught at school or university. And I had to learn everything again—language, culture, and everyday life.

By this time I had already managed to make friends with Andy. We often went out downtown on Saturday nights.

4

Christmas was approaching, and I called Daniela. I wanted to know what she would do at Christmas. Daniela said that she was taking her Christmas holidays in Latvia. I did wish her a good time at home prior to her departure. She came to see me, and I wanted to give her Christmas presents for Mom and Emily.

Andy asked me if I would like spend Christmas together with him and attend his family's Christmas dinner. I asked him to tell his parents and relatives. Andy replied that they all knew and would like to meet me.

I was afraid of what they would say, but it turned out that my fears were totally unfounded. Andy introduced me to the family, and I was made to feel welcome. Andy's family was very warmhearted and hospitable.

Unlike Latvia, in Ireland the holy day is celebrated on Christmas Day, not Christmas Eve. A traditional dinner is stuffed turkey and pork ham, Brussels cabbage and cranberry sauce, and sweet strawberry trifle with three sweet cake layers and strawberry jelly at the bottom, a middle layer of custard, whipped cream, and decorated on the top with fruit. At lunch, there was white and red wine, with ice cream, tea, and coffee afterwards.

After lunch, we all moved into the living room. Andy came from a large family, with six boys and three girls. Andy watched his mom with admiration, cope with the children. Sometimes I was not able to cope with one, and she had nine. However, Andy's mom, it seems, was not at all affected. In her there was something noble and you could see that she was able to maintain her emotional balance. She literally exuded grace and peace, although she probably did not find it easy to raise their children, while her husband was away working in England.

Some of Andy's relatives worked outside Ireland—two brothers in England, one in Australia, and one of the sisters in Scotland.

All the children now arrived back home for Christmas vacation. The afternoon passed fast. We all agreed to meet later. Andy said, "I will see you later in town, down at the pub."

The Christmas holiday was gone quickly, and I went back to work. Time was running. Spring arrived unnoticed. Finally, in the village a vacant house came up for rent. Diana and I moved into the village house on the main street.

On the first floor, next door were a vegetable shop and a notary. The house was large and old, built in 1900, with two floors. The first floor had a large kitchen, which was modernized, but the old stone floor remained, and the living room had an old fireplace from 1930.

The second floor had four bedrooms, two in the middle, and two smaller ones, one on each side. Outside the street was noisy from 5:00 a.m. until 2:00 a.m. next morning.

Traffic was nonstop, with lorries, pedestrians, cars, and buses. The house was much too big for us two. Nevertheless, we left the nursing home. Living there felt like work, with no break.

The homeowner said he didn't mind if we had subtenants. It would make it easier to pay all charges and utility bills. It was not a bad idea. However, how would we get anyone to share the house?

We decided to advertise in the store window, the post office, and on the credit union message board. Within two years the house had a number of tenants. Our house was the first stepping stone for many Latvians, a temporary residence while they got on their feet, got a job and apartment, and got stabilized.

My relationship with Andy had become serious, more than a friendship, and we decided we would move in together in an attempt to live together. For me, it was a very responsible step, because after my divorce I swore to myself that I would never have another relationship with a man. But with Andy, it was different. He was brought up differently; he always treated me with respect, understanding, and tolerance.

He realized that I had been through hardship and it would take time for my wounds to heal.

In the autumn, we found a small house outside the village, about ten minutes by foot, five with the car. We bought our first car, and we decided how much money each of us would give for our household expenses.

Therefore, we started a new family life of cohabitation. I did not have the slightest notion what Andy liked and didn't like.

This proved two things—friendship and life together with people of other nationalities are two different things.

However, I loved this man very much. I put all my efforts into understanding Andy with all my heart and soul.

I tried to keep my eyes and ears open, and quickly adapt to the new lifestyle. I was not a bad cook; we did not have any disagreement about our menu. Also, I was trying to be careful in choosing products that we both liked.

When we were visiting Andy's parents, I watched Andy's mom preparing dinner and learned how to cook Irish dinners. Gradually I tried to learn the Irish domestic routine. On Saturday and Sunday, we rested together. My English was also slowly developing.

On the August bank holiday, I went along with Andy and his friends to the Aran Islands. Ireland was a marvelous country, with landscapes and the ocean, islands, and mountains. It was a beautiful paradise.

We spent a marvelous vacation. When we were heading back home, our relationship became very close. I was happy, very happy. I wanted to get pregnant and give Andy a baby. I was desperate, because I knew that it was an unrealistic aim. I saw that Andy longed for a family and children. Andy loved children and was very good with them. Andy's nephew and nieces adored him.

I felt uncomfortable, because seven years ago after surgery for ovarian cancer, doctors told me that I was unlikely to have any more children. With one ovary, it was almost impossible to become pregnant. It pushed me over the edge.

I tried to talk to Andy about it, but we did not have a good conversation. Probably I chose the wrong time to talk. On the other hand, we did not know how to openly speak about this matter.

Employed by a nursing home, I was emotionally attached to the people living there, and it was not a good sign. It is not a professional attitude to the work, if you are attached to your patients emotionally.

They were all old people. And spending every day at work with your partner is not the best option either. I decided to change my occupation. I mentioned to Andy that I would like to change jobs, trying to explain the reason. He had no objections. In one of the village's supermarket there was a notice that they were recruiting new staff members for work. I applied for an interview. The reply said that the management would get back to me.

I kept on working in the nursing home. I really liked working here, but I got very upset when someone died.

In early October, someone called me on my cell phone and said that the director wanted to see me. Could I make the appointment? I answered that I would. I called Andy to say that the Super Value director asked me for another interview. He wished me success, and said good-bye. "See you in evening." I was going to the village for the interview.

The owner was very kind, and asked me a few questions. Had I ever worked in a shop? I said that I had worked in a shop very long time ago, during my studies. And I would like to be among people and work in a team with people. He asked when I could start work; I said any time, even tomorrow.

The director determined the date and time I would need to be at work. Thus, my emotional dependency problem was solved. I loved having set hours, five days a week, from Monday to Friday, 8:00 a.m. to 5:00 p.m., Saturdays and Sundays were free. The salary was not as high as in the retirement home, but I would have more time for Andy and myself for our new family.

The job was more interesting, with more people around, and I liked it. My colleagues were very nice, and village people were friendly. It was nice to live and work in a place that you loved and liked to be.

In autumn, I decided to study in the local college and get a degree in business studies and marketing. And I was happy that Andy did not mind Diana joining me for college. She wanted to choose nursing, to study to become a medical administrator. The classes were two times a week, Tuesday and Thursday evenings from 6:00 p.m. to 9:00 p.m. In addition, sessions on Saturdays were from 10:00 a.m. to 4:00 p.m.

Diana's training classes were held on Monday evenings and Fridays, so we saw each other very rarely. Each of us developed our separate lives. Work, family, and studies took up all my time.

My work visa came at the end of the deadline to submit documents for renewal. From the Immigration and Labor Department came a letter that the passport maturity is too short, and there was only six months left to renew the work visa. If I wanted to renew a work permit, then I had to first renew my passport. The passport's validity was expiring in six months, too.

This was an unexpected turn. There were two options, to either go to England, to the Latvian embassy and get a new passport in London, or go to Latvia. Everything had to be thoroughly considered and I had to figure out the better option. If I went to England, it might take a month before the Latvian passport arrived, and during this time I would have to live in London. It could be very expensive. It might be better to go Latvia. Tickets were expensive, but the passport renewal would take only two weeks. I could visit my mother and my daughter and spend that time with them.

I decided to go to Latvia, and to take formal leave from work. I explained the pros and cons to my boss and started to prepare for travel. I asked Andy to take his annual holidays and go with me to Latvia. He said that now he could not take a vacation. Well, I would go alone. Andy accompanied me to the airport. On the way there, we visited his relatives in Dublin.

Two weeks was a long time, and it would give us the opportunity to examine ourselves and our relationship. The first week in Latvia passed quickly, while the next week went slowly. I already wanted to go back home. I had a conversation with Emily. After Emily completed her technician course, she would come over to Ireland to live with us. We would send her a ticket. I shared my joy about being happy with Andy with my mother and Emily. They were interested in everything, how we met, how we got on with his parents and relatives at Christmas dinner, our relationship, plans, and whether it was serious between us. I said that it looked like it was serious. Andy called me almost every day in Latvia, and I had already started to miss him. It looked like it was very serious, at least on my part.

The passport was issued, and I went back to Ireland. Andy's mom said that Andy looked unlucky, deserted, and lost. He was expecting me back home. I confessed to her that I was missing him. I was back at home, and I was happy to be back.

How little people need to feel happy. I was back at work and school, and life took its familiar rhythm. We loved each other, and Andy was an invaluable aid for me in learning to speak good English. He pointed out my grammatical errors so that I would not repeat the same mistakes during conversation. My boss at work suggested that I speak slowly. "You do not realize that you are talking too fast, and it is difficult for customers to understand what you are saying. Your knowledge of English is good—just speak slowly and clearly so that local people can understand you."

Time passed, and all was well, but on my next vacation in Latvia, I went to see experts to talk about my options for becoming pregnant. The doctor expressed his personal opinion. "If you want a baby so much, you have to pray to the Lord. Sometimes miracles happen." It left me frustrated.

When I arrived home, I did not say anything about my unfortunate visit to the doctors. Men do not understand those things. These were my problems and it might be that it was just my thought that we should have children. They say that it is a natural process that women have always wanted impossible and unattainable.

One night, I saw in Andy's face an expression of boredom. I ask him, "What happened?"

The answer is, "Nothing. I am going down to see my mother." I can see that he is bored. Andy is accustomed to being around kids all the time. He was leaving to go visit his parents.

I went outside get some fresh air. It was quiet, and there were stars in the sky. I saw an asteroid falling. In childhood we believed that if you saw a star falling and you wanted something with all your heart, then you made a wish on the falling star, and the wish would come true. "Tell him, oh, God, please do something so that I can became pregnant, that I can give Andy a baby. You see that he is very fond of children, and I want to make him happy, please, please, really, really, from all my heart and soul."

We continued to live together, going to school, work, home, with tours on Saturdays or Sundays. We traveled to all the nearest beautiful places; we went to the ocean. We went to the Cliffs of Mother. I stood on the edge of the cliff. It was amazing. You could actually feel the magnificence of the ocean. You felt the power of eternity as you stood there, and got this feeling of rising up to the sky. When you closed your eyes, you had the sensation of flying. It was a beautiful sensation of freedom and universal energy.

We drove to visit my old workmates on the mushroom farm. Several old employees were gone—they found other work—but still one or two were there, and new ones had come. I introduced Andy to my sister, and she and Andy found a common language very easily; they both were on the same wavelength. Andy asked Daniela if she liked picking mushrooms. My sister, laughing, said that it was an interesting question. Then she said she would love to do something else, but now there was nothing that might be available or suitable for her.

Andy was surprised to learn that Daniela was an artist. He said that he could not understand us. Daniela explained to him that at the moment in Latvia painting could not earn you bread, if you were not a celebrity. People did not buy paintings, and she had no money, so she came to Ireland. As soon as Daniela could find something suitable, a decorator job or an artist job, she would stop picking mushrooms. We had a nice day together.

5

In October, I started to feel sick, nauseated, tired, and nervous, with a headache. My period was running late, so I bought a pregnancy test.

I was pregnant. I looked at the test monitor and could not believe my own eyes. Was I seeing it clearly or was I having phantom hallucinations? I would have a baby, Andy's baby. I called Andy, and I could not stay calm.

I phoned Diana and told her the news. She was very happy for me. She knew that I wanted a baby very much.

I called my mom and my sister and told them I was pregnant. They doubt it. "Are you sure? You know that it is impossible in your situation with one ovary." Yes, I knew—the doctor was right that, even these days, miracles still happened.

Andy returned from work and asked me, "What did you say on the phone?"

I repeated one more time, "I'm pregnant—we will have a baby."

He said slowly, "Bunny, but you said that you cannot have children."

I replied, "The doctors told me that after surgery!"

We were both very happy, but so far, we decided to say nothing until the doctor confirmed that everything was in order, that I was pregnant, and that the baby was okay. In midsummer, I gave birth by Caesarean section to our daughter, Sarah. She was a healthy and perfect baby. Our happiness was complete.

Emily finished technical college and came over to Ireland to live with us. My two daughters both were home with me. Emily went to work as a nurse assistant at a nursing home to improve her English language skills, and gain practical work experience prior to admission to a medical college. Both of my daughters were with me, and I was the happiest person in the world.

Andy and I decided to become engaged, which meant that I was his chosen bride, and that we would get married after a year. We started to save money for wedding expenses. Everyone was very happy.

An announcement that we were engaged and would be getting married was made to the family. We explained that we were getting married in a year's time, when Sarah was a bit older.

That winter was very harsh, cold, rainy, and with severe cases of a virus, suffered by children and old people. Also, Andy and Emily got sick, but for them it was a matter of days, and once the doctor prescribed medication, everything was fine.

Sarah got a very complicated form of the disease when she was just six months old, caused by high fever, and she started to get convulsions.

We called the doctor. Our family doctor said that as a result of high temperature Sarah developed severe epilepsy. He referred us to the district general hospital. We immediately went there. The hospital casualty department sent us to the children's ward. There we were greeted by the nurse, who said that the doctor would be with us now to investigate Sarah.

Suddenly she fell sick and started shaking. Her face and body turned blue. The nurse quickly grabbed the girl and ran away. We were confused and did not understand what was happening. The nurse came back to us, and told us to go to the parents' waiting room.

We waited for something to happen. I felt like we had been there ages. Finally the doctor came to us and said that little Sarah had just gone through a very strong epileptic seizure. It was so strong that Sara's life was threatened, but now everything was over and our little daughter was relaxing. It was difficult for the mind to comprehend—epilepsy, from whom?

The doctor said, "The cause of the attacks is unknown. Sarah will need to undergo a number of tests and checks. Maybe then we will be able to tell you what is wrong with her." The fits repeated the next day. She was connected to an oxygen supply.

The doctors started Sarah on epilepsy medicine. I was confused and Sarah started a long journey through tests, tests, and more tests, which showed nothing. Sarah was a healthy, perfect child. She did not have any abnormalities or mutations. Everything was in perfect order. Four months were spent in hospitals.

Fortunately, the doctors, nurses, and support personnel at Republican Children's Hospital and the district general hospital were highly experienced and professional, and their attitude was friendly and affectionate. We had all kinds of endless analysis and a variety of the most advanced tests. But the cause was still unclear.

Sara's health improved, and the medicine helped us to return home. Her seizures were under control. We did not notice the arrival of spring, green and blooming.

The weather was warm, and Sarah and I were spending lot of time outdoors, walking in the fresh air.

Walking with Sarah, we met our priest William at the church. I thanked him for finding time for us and being so kind to come visit us at the hospital in Dublin. He asked, "How are you? How Sarah is doing? Does Sarah feel better?" He was very tactful and empathic. I saw that he could be trusted.

We started talk. I did not belong to any religion, but Andy and I wanted Sarah to be christened and brought up in the Catholic faith. I asked his opinion; he said that Sarah was important. Father William asked Andy and me to come up to his place to discuss and agree on Sarah's christening date. As much for me, who never had any dealings with religion, William said he would ask Sister Joan to be my religion teacher and explain to me the importance of the sacraments, to prepare me for this important event in my life and my daughter's christening.

The next time when I see him, I asked, "Why was God so cruel to my little daughter and me? I wanted Sarah so badly, she was born a healthy baby, but he let her get this terrible disease. Why did he make my baby so sick? Why? If he wanted me to punish me for my sins, why did he not take any action against me, why against Sarah? She is just an innocent baby! Why should she have to suffer for her parents' sins?"

William told me that I was very wrong! This was not the work of God or the Lord's revenge. God would not hurt the feelings of another person. God is unconditional, infinite love; he even gave his son so that we could live without sin, and eternal love. The pastor said that he understood very well how I felt, how desperate, and how much it saddens me, but God never wanted this suffering, and did not want Sarah to get sick. He would never hurt innocent children, and the only thing I could do was to ask him to help Sarah recover, and to help the doctor find the cause of her illness, and to find appropriate treatment.

A mother's prayer has great power. I felt uncomfortable; I knew that I went too far. The next time I went for a walk with Sarah, I went to church. I sat down on the bench and tried to concentrate to pray. I could not. My mind went blank, enabling my emotions to shake out all the accumulated pain in my heart. I was in tears. My despair was going through the air; I asked God for forgiveness, for the undeserved insults on my part. I said that I was distraught and that I was really hurt that my little one had to suffer so much and I could not help her with anything. She was twitching in my arms and I could not do anything to ease her suffering. I begged Jesus Christ so that he would help my daughter, so that she would recover and stay healthy. I begged him to give me the strength to fight through it all, to be strong and durable, so I would be able to hide my pain and tears in front of others. My job was to be strong and to keep others' hope alive that everything would be fine. I asked God to give me strength not to be desperate and not to lose hope and faith!

Sara's baptism was here. It was a wonderful day, the sun rolling on the earth. The ceremony was very beautiful, moving, and important. Four events in human life in Ireland are significant—baptism, first Holy Communion, weddings, and funerals. All of them are important parts of a person's life.

After some time, Andy and I noticed that Sarah was stuck in her development. Physically she was growing taller, but there was no change in her development. She did not play or show interest in anything. We were concerned.

In the next visit to the pediatrician, we expressed our concerns about Sarah's overall development. The doctor promised to send us to professionals to do an assessment of her general development. Our concerns were justified. Sarah's development had stopped when she experienced a life-threatening, strong epileptic seizure.

I could not even firmly express in words how painful it was for me. Behind the big emotions there was a twinge in my chest, choking me. My heart broke apart because of the pain of my poor little baby.

I went to church, and I was confused. Desperately I asked Jesus Christ for advice. "Please tell me, what I can do? I implore you to have mercy on my child and help her. Please help her to recover!" Sarah was put on a special list for children with special needs. Ireland had an organization that took care of such children and their parents, called "Jack and Jill." Once a month a nurse came to the house from this organization.

It was a great aid in the beginning because I was so confused that I did not know what to do. The nurse was trained to give moral support and advice on where to go for your situation, and the right person to turn to for help.

One thing was clear, I could forget about studying and my career. My attention had to be devoted to little Sarah's recovery. The nurse said that it was not quite so drastic that I couldn't try to commit to part-time work and continuing education online. I gave up my work in the super-store. However, life at home was boring. Sarah spent a lot of time sleeping and I was on my own most of the time. Andy was at work all day. It did not suit me, and I felt depressed and lonely.

I got a phone call from Diana. She had moved to Galway and worked in a large hospital as an administrator's assistant. She said, "I called to say I miss you. Would you like to come visit me?" I went with Sarah.

I was so glad to see an old friend. It is so good to talk with someone who knows you and understands, and you don't have to put on a brave face. Diana told me that they often required a hospital interpreter who could translate from Latvian into English, as an interpreter in Russian-English.

The interpreter agency was looking for people with a good command of English, knowledge, and experience. It was on-call work, which meant that I would not have to be at work every day, but only when there was a need. I got the phone number of the agencies from Diana. Back home I told Andy the news and said that I would be happy to work if he had no objections. He said to call the agency and ascertain whether they are willing to take me on. I called the agency and was invited for a job interview.

The agency offered me the interpreter's job, but it appeared that little Sarah had other plans. She flatly refused to eat when someone else tried to feed her, and did not drink for anybody else. We found a professional babysitter. Sarah refused to eat and drink outside the home. We hired a babysitter at home, but nothing changed. Sarah still refused to be fed by somebody else. Sarah recognized me and was able to distinguish differences between family and outsiders. Andy tried to feed her, and Sarah opened her mouth, but kept the food in her mouth and would not swallow. As soon as Andy took his eyes from her, everything was back out.

She already had made up her mind. I had to give up the interpreting work and take full-time care of our daughter.

After a bit I became more familiar with the new situation, and Andy and I got back to wedding planning. Soon there a year had passed since our engagement.

Emily meanwhile moved to Derry, in Northern Ireland. She got a job in a shop, met a person, and they became friends. Emily would come to our wedding with her boyfriend, to introduce him to the family.

From my side the wedding guests would be my mom, sister, daughter, and some Latvians, my former colleagues and acquaintances. From Andy's side would be his relatives, family, friends, and colleagues. Then there were the neighbors, nuns, and priests.

The wedding took place in a large hotel. The wedding guests numbered about two hundred people. Everything was very beautiful and nice, only I was saddened that, on my side, only a few of the invited guests attended. I tried to be a good woman of the house and greet all the guests.

When the wedding party ended, I sat down at the bar. I was tired. The bartender asked me what was pressing on my heart and mind. I said that I was upset about those who did not come. The bartender told me, "Stop worrying about silly things. Do not be sad for those who did not come—it is not worth it. Rejoice for those who have arrived—they are your real friends who wish you both the best. Those are many more than you think." It made me rethink my attitude.

Indeed, ever since I had started to go out with Andy, and then Sarah's birth, a lot had changed in my life. I was estranged from local Latvians, who did not like that my husband was an Irishman, or that I was tied to home and did not participate in any activities or have time for friends. I really did not have any extra time for friends or extended family.

My whole life was subordinate to the needs of my daughter, her appointments at the doctors, and her procedures. I did not look for any friendships. Only when someone needed to fill out an application form, or had to phone and arrange a meeting, or something in English, did the local Latvians contact me. The only person with whom I had contact on a regular basis was my very first friend, with whom I worked from day one, and who is still my friend.

After the wedding, I was a married woman and had to change my passport to my new family name. Thank goodness I did not have to go to Latvia. In 2004, Latvia was admitted to the European Union, and in Ireland there were quite a number of Latvians who lived and worked there.

Latvian government opened a consulate in Dublin, which was handy. When my mum was visiting us, I took her and Sarah and we all three went to Dublin. We found the address of the Latvian Embassy, and we went there. When we arrived at the building, I was unpleasantly surprised. At the high gate was a queue. People had been in the queue since 7:00 a.m. Business hours turned out to be from 10:30 a.m. until 1:00 p.m., from Monday to Friday—two and a half hours a day. Only ten visitors were allowed to enter through the gate at a time.

I was trying to reach the security guard standing at the side of the gate, to explain that I had an emergency—that I had a sick child with me and could not afford to stand for hours in a queue.

The security guards at the entrance said that it was not a problem if others who were waiting did not object. They could let us through the gate immediately.

I moved up to the raised ladder and turned to the people waiting in the queue. "My dear compatriots! Friends! I now need to change my passport after my wedding as I am now a married woman and I have another family name. I brought my little girl with me who has epilepsy, and my mom, who came to Ireland for my wedding. She helps me today with the buggy and my child. If I cannot submit the paperwork today, I will have to wait until my mother will be able to come back next year.

"Do you object if we get into the top ten? For me it is the only application submission, and I hope that we will not delay anybody too much. Is someone willing to let us to the front of the queue?" No one had any objection, and we were let to the front of the queue. People in the queue, regardless of their own problems, were sensitive and understanding.

The atmosphere in the consulate was unpleasant. The lobby secretary seated at the table was the pinnacle of vanity and contempt. Sitting at the table, the young woman showed a clear reluctance that I had disturbed her beauty grooming session. I asked her, "Where I can get a passport application form?" It was unpleasant to see that this young woman was convinced that this work site, this embassy, had been created especially for her so she could live comfortably and pleasantly. This snobbery was common in Latvia. I had already managed to forget this unpleasant feature because usually when you were in one of the Irish authorities, the treatment was pleasant, and people were interested in helping to solve your problem.

This young woman in her snobbery refused to understand that she should be grateful to the Irish Latvians that she had the privilege of working abroad, and a good salary, because if we did not come to work here, and there were not so many, then there would not be a Latvian consulate, and she might sit in the secretariat of some African country or in the secretariat of the ministry, running off her feet. The welcoming attitude towards visitors and potential clients should be an integral part of professionalism.

In any case, she was pathetic. What is worth learning and wisdom, the heart of the person is a piece of ice. The receptionist answered a telephone call, and her English accent was terrible. It was shameful that we had such people representing Latvian interests abroad. It presented a very unpleasant image.

So, finally, I found the Passport Department. Women here were the complete opposite of the employee sitting in the lobby. They should have switched locations, so as not to damage the first impression of the embassy. Unlike the lobby receptionist-secretary, the passport department employee was kind, polite, and highly professional in her work. We decided that my passport would be sent to by mail to me at home, and I took full responsibility if anything happened to it, if it got damaged or lost.

On the second trip with small, sick children, in long queues, maybe next time we would not be so lucky and accommodated by my compatriots. It could be risky. I decided the "Latvian mood" was not my style; it caused me uncomfortable stomach cramps.

I hoped that after the next twenty-five years the atmosphere and the attitude of the people who have consular staff jobs and wages would be changed. Maybe simple country folk would get a little bit of respect, which they deserve as Latvian citizens, and not treated as begging tramps in the eyes of Latvian elite class snobs.

Years went by. We noticed the first signs of life beginning to appear in Sarah's development. Maybe my prayers would eventually be answered. We all have a hidden desire and dreams. Often they are related to the financial well-being and wealth. In addition, probably it is hard to imagine that we ourselves are the greatest treasure. We want more, which is no great pool of real values, the things without which we can do: big houses, which we are not even able to manage by ourselves, so we have to hire special employees; fast, modern cars, which are often the cause of accidents; lots of money, which causes conflicts in the family.

At the same time, we take for granted the ability to walk, to talk, to laugh, and to be able to take care of ourselves. We take health, the ability to have control of your own life, free will, and choice as part of ourselves from birth, not realizing that it's all God-given treasure, and it is our real value.

Only when we face life with disease or without abilities do we realize how much we take for granted and do not appreciate the real value of the ability to see, hear, talk, walk, and enjoy life.

We pray to God for things that we really do not need. When we ask for something that we really need now, our prayers are answered, and we are given what we need.

Preparing for Sarah's baptism, I made friends with Sister Joanna. She was a very intelligent and educated nun. I could discuss any issues of interest to me with her.

I had looked for years for my place in life. It seemed that finally I had found it. Sarah has brought light and love to my life. I never could understand what the expression unconditional love meant. Now I knew it. It seemed to me that it was the love that I felt for my baby. When I held her in my hands, I felt that tenderness and love shining and radiating from Sarah. And I did not need anything more.

I knew that she knew that I loved her with all my heart and soul. In my life, I had never loved anybody so much as this little miracle of God, this precious baby. And I was willing to take care of her for as long as needed, even to the end of my life.

My only prayer to God was, "Jesus Christ, please give my child the ability to heal, to recover in the spirit and the flesh. Just give her the ability to walk, run, play ball, laugh, and enjoy her childhood as well as all other children. God, Lord give her understanding that she would be able to feed herself, take care about herself, so that when the time comes for me to leave this world, so I can go with peace in my heart, and I know that Sarah is able to take care of herself and not depend on other people's charity. Oh, God, give me patience and health this day."

I accepted the Catholic faith and became a Catholic. Jesus Christ had done so much for me that I had no reason to doubt his existence and love for me. I could not imagine life without him, without his love for me.

Sarah began to develop. She started to attend preschool, and an after-school program. Her epileptic seizures remained much lighter, and if she was healthy, she could go 3–5 weeks without any seizure.

Sarah was able to express her likes and dislikes, to express her emotions with facial expressions and her eyes.

She was able to sit up for quite a long time. We still had problems with eating. Sarah still had to take many drugs and not have an appetite. She had sleep disorders, but the girl's health improved, and I knew, I just knew it in my heart that one day she would stand up and walk.

And my prayer to God was that the Lord would give me the strength not to despair, but to keep alive the hope and faith that my child would be one day cured. "Amen!"

Sarah turned eight years old, and we celebrated her first Holy Communion. She received her first Holy Communion together with other children from our residential community. The sun was shining. We were so proud of her. In spite of all her sufferings, she was here in our church together with other children. She had come so far already.

After Sarah's first Holy Communion, I met with Father William-Pierre and we had a little chat. "Lolita, I noticed that you were trying to keep yourself calm, but tears were in your eyes. Why?" Father William asked me.

"I really do not know. Every time something is going on, I am in tears. They are coming out from my eyes by themselves. I have no control over it."

"Do you know what I think? You are trying to be strong, and keeping everything inside you. You have it out, get it off your chest. Share it—people will understand it!"

"No, I can't! I do not want anyone to know what I have gone through." I defiantly refused to share my feelings with anybody.

"Write it down," Father William suggested. "That way you do not have to talk about it, but people still can read it. Your knowledge could be somebody's salvation."

Father William left, and I returned to the church to say thank you to Christ. I knelt for the prayer.

I saw a vision of Sarah running. We were all at the house, outside with Sarah and two more children—a girl and a boy with blond hair. Sarah was wearing her white dress and she was holding a white ball in her hands. My husband was beside me and he had his arm around my shoulders. All the family was there. It was a party. My mother was sitting at the table on the lawn. At the next table were my parents-in-law. My sisters-in-law were standing with wine glasses and chatting in a circle.

I came out of the trance. Everything was so clear. I believed that Sarah one day would enjoy her childhood. I knew as long I believed and kept faith, as long I tried to do my best, my daughter would thrive on my love.

www.ingramcontent.com/pod-product-compliance
Lightning Source LLC
Chambersburg PA
CBHW071235280526
45787CB00002B/939